I Am

Somebody

By Quay Boddie

KeniAH,
thank you
for everything!

Published by
www.ebooksolutions.org

Contents

#1

(Down but Not Out)

Lost some but the game is not over!
Setbacks but comebacks are on the way!
Been talked about but that doesn't phase me!
Once it's all said and done, I'll be back like I never left.
Step aside I'm coming through step to the left!

#2

(Not the same)

I'm different and that's a fact.
I'm not the stereotype and never will I act.
Gifts and talent are running wild on the inside.
God gave it to me so I can't hide.
Anything different I won't claim.
I'm not what you are used too.
I'm not the same.

#3

(Effort)

It's all on you
Nobody can give it to you
Nobody can take it away
A little bit goes a long way
Today, how much will put out?

#4

(No Secret)

It's not rocket science!
Don't wreck your brain trying to figure it
out!
It's simple!
Be you and stay true!
You want to know how to live your life?
Live it how you want to and that's to the
fullest!
THERE IS NO SECRET!

#5

(You)

Nothing can come against you!
There are plans in place for you!
Things being done that you know
nothing about.
You aren't worthless and you have
purpose.

#6

(Behind the scenes)

They don't know the work you put
in.
They don't understand you.
They have not seen the sweat.
They have not seen the tears.
They don't know about the sacrifices
made.
It's all been behind the scenes!

#7

(With Him)

With Him I can't lose!
*I can conquer the world
*I can dream
*I can have
With Him is life!

#8

(Arms Reach)

It's not far away,
Did you know that?
It's always been yours to grab!
For the longest time you have
stretched yourself,
You've done this for what reason?
Just to give up?!!
I think not! What you have been in
pursuit for is in arms reach!
DON'T FORGET THAT!

#9

(Placement)

Life will take you here and life will take you there but remember that there is a place for you. Our worst thing ever is always thinking we fit in where we may not belong. Trust in the placement that is to come.

#10

(In Return)

You get in what you put out. So if you get nothing then don't pout! It's better to give then receive I hope that's something you believe and learn. You get what you give and if that's nothing then there will be nothing in return.

#11

(Bare Minimum)

Bare minimum makes you.....
*Like everyone else
*Complacent
*Lazy
Anybody can do bare minimum but
why cheat yourself?

#12

(Called)

Your calling in life doesn't move unless you move within your life. Its ok if you missed that, I will break it down for you. You may not see or understand this particular season of your life. It's all a part of the "calling" process. God will place you right where you need to be and He will show you some things. Blessings will fall right into place but it's up to you to protect it when your calling comes to full affect.

#13

(They don't love you)

They put on and pretend but do they really have your back? They may say I'll love you to end but leave you in the wind. Either way you can live without em. I hope you know this!

#14

(Match)

Understand this: Some people will never be able to match your energy and character. You may be consistent with your character and truth and they may not be able to handle you or what you bring to the table. Be ok with that.

#15

(D.T.J.D.)

"Don't talk, just do it!" If you are who you say and serve the God almighty above then people will automatically see your worth and quality. You won't have to prove points because actions speak for themselves. Being the best of the best is just one of many perks to being a child of the most high. You better recognize!

#16

(Set the example)

We should "set examples" not being the examples! For instance, who really enjoys going to jail?
We should "set examples" on how to not end up in jail through positive acts. Being the example means you have ignored the positive examples that could have been set. BE SMART!

#17

(You just know)

There is a feeling you get when you know the lord is going to bless you. It's a feeling you can't explain and an experience you will never forget. You have been through so much that nobody can change your mindset. "You just know" God is on the way.

#18

(Expecting)

Expecting can be a good thing but then a bad thing as well. Always expecting that someone will do and treat you like you do is not how you should think. On another note, expecting that great things are coming along for you and your life (because they will) is the way to be and will help you overcome.

#19

(Be the man)

Be the man who takes care of his
family!
Be the man who is the gentleman!
Be the man you would want your
son to be like!
Be the man you would want your
daughter to date!
Be the man who respects himself at
all times!
Be the man who makes it happen!

#20

(Be the woman)

Be the woman who keeps the house together!
Be the woman who is the definition of a lady!
Be the woman who respects herself and body!
Be the woman that sets the example for all women!
Be the woman who is a go getta!

#21

(Respect)

It's a give and take. You have to give it to get it! It goes a very long way! It will save you in select situations. It is appreciated on many levels. How far would you go with or without being on the giving or receiving end of it?

#22

(Not only for you)

Yes, take care of you but remember that you don't only live for you. Be careful and mindful that you represent your friends, family, and loved ones as well. Watch what you say and watch what you do because when it's all said and done just remember you live for more than just you.

CHECKPOINT!

As my good friend Megan Ware would say, you are beautifully and wonderfully made and that's all to the Lord's doing. No matter how you look. No matter your shape. No matter your condition. You are important! You are blessed and highly favored! When you look into the mirror today be reminded of who you are and why you are here.

CHECKPOINT!

As my good friend Daniel Walker would say; "there isn't anything wrong with being a man and loving God!" Most men today think that just because you love God that you are weak! I will tell you first hand without God in my life, I don't know where I would be! So, I am going to praise Him because He holds me! If anything, you become stronger as a man with power that the Lord gives you! DON'T BE ASHAMED!

#23

(Give her something better!)

She has been through hell and back. She has been heart broken. She has been lied to. She has been crushed. She has been run over and had countless nights with lost sleep. She has doubted herself. What she needs is something different. She needs it done the right way; someone who won't mess around with her. GIVE HER SOMETHING BETTER!

#24

(Destroy you)

Your enemies and the devil don't play fair. They know that you are capable of good so they try to make you do badly. They want to make the word "potential" not even exist. They want to make the word "success" not even exist. What you have to do is come prepared for this thing called life. If you come unprepared "life" will chew you up and spit you out! It's plain and simple, don't be destroyed!

#25

(In the midst)

He is with you always.
He has never left you and never will.
Don't be scared and don't you fear.
God is in the midst, He is here.

#26

(Just Ask)

You never know a person's story! Try not to beat them down. You don't ever know what to expect. Be careful of how you treat others. Rough issues hit us all and that makes us down and out. "Just ask" someone what's going on, prayer is great for others and will help them out.

#27

(Say and Act)

Time after time we always say "I know God is on my side." "I know that I am covered." "I know that it's all going to work out." What's the purpose of saying all these things if we are acting like these things aren't true? BECAUSE THEY ARE! Running around looking crazy and stressed solves nothing!

#28

(Marathon)

Why sprint through life? Think about your pace. Things won't always come quick like a sprint. It's ok to take your time and flow with the marathon! Within the sprint can be trouble, things you don't want, and things you don't need. Within the marathon you may have frustration at times but when it's all said and done you will appreciate that you cared enough to be patient and learn lessons

#29

(Lost in the fire)

Don't get caught up so much in life's trials. It's easy to lose focus on what is important due to things happening around you. It's easy to run away when you don't feel like dealing with something that bothers you. It's easy to compromise and do things you wouldn't usually do. Hang in there don't go down get higher and never get lost in the fire!

#30

(Connected)

Like pieces to a puzzle
Like bones joined in the body
Like Lego pieces making a shape
If you have a relationship with the
most high then you can relate. Get
connected! Stay connected!

#31

(Everybody)

Coach would always say "if it was easy then everybody could/would do it!" Everybody is not as talented as you! Everybody can't do what you do! So, the next time you question why you do what you do just know everybody can't be like you.

#32

(Hot Commodity)

You're rare
You're original
You aren't the norm
You're a gentleman
You're a lady
You're smart
You're attractive
You're selfless
You're humble
You're a lover
You're a shining light
You're who they want to be around,
you got it going on!

#33

(In the end)

Lord it does get tough but I trust
you!
Sometimes I want to give up!
Sometimes I question what I am even
doing?
Sometimes I fall but I know it will all
fall into place.

#34

(Stamp it!)

Just as you go to the post office to mail a letter, it can't be sent without a stamp! Put a stamp on your hopes, dreams, and aspirations. This is called declaring and decreeing that you understand how important it is to speak life and not death. Stamp it today and send it off!

#35

(Line Up!)

Don't count yourself out! You are in line for what you have waited for, hoped for, and prayed for! Stay in line!

#36

(Repetitive Nature)

You gain things in your life through a "Repetitive Nature!" The more you try God time after time you will gain. The more you step out on faith you will be gaining. The more you work at your craft or gift you have been blessed with, you will be gaining. God won't let you fail! Become repetitive for growth.

#37

(Do we wait?)

Remember in grade school when you liked a certain guy or girl? You would take a sheet of paper and on it "you want to be my girlfriend/ boyfriend?" (Yes, no, maybe) You would wait all day for a reply hoping they said yes. You had high hopes because you wanted that person badly. What I'm trying to say is if we can wait and have hope/ patience back then with our young selves; why can't we do it now with our grown selves. Hold on because either way God provides you with the best outcome.

#38

(Checklist)

What do you take with you daily? Before you walk out of the house daily there are things that are vital to make your day go a lot smoother. I want you to add something for me to your Checklist if not already there...

#1 Have a will and a want to be something and do something above the norm.

#2 Have crazy faith that no matter what you won't lose sight of what you are going after. (It's going to happen)

#3 Have the mindset to adapt and overcome because things change and happen but don't let that slow you down or stop you!

#39

(Listen Up!)

At this current time you may be down and out but don't tell me that you don't know how to get back up! You probably have been knocked down before so, what makes this time any different? Implant this word in your mind and don't forget it "UNDEFEATED!"

You can't be stopped and won't be stopped from now on! Who or what in their right mind thinks they can stop you with God? VICTORIOUS! Watch out world, you have an overcomer on the rise!

#40

(Train Still Boarding)

You have not missed your train!
There is still time to board!
*Being Complacent
*Being Doubtful
*Being weak minded
*Being affected by current situations
has made you believe that your
blessings will be no more. Didn't
God say that He would never leave
you nor forsake you? GET ON THE
TRAIN!

#41

(Do Better)

I don't know about you but I can remember as a kid doing something I had no business doing. As my grandmother approached me she would say "boy you know better than that!" What I'm saying is today since we know better let's do better!

#42

(I shout)

I will shout in the beginning when I am just getting started. I will shout when I am on top! Your shout symbolizes that you won't lay down! LET'S HEAR IT!

#43

(But)

Have you ever noticed in every conversation there is always a "but?"
*But......
-My bills are due
-I just lost my job
-When will I get over this illness?
-I'm scared
In this case "but" is a word used while worrying.
*But....Did you know that there is no issue to big or small for the ALMIGHTY!

#44

(When You Are Fed Up!)

When you are tired of being broke. When you are not where you want to be in life. If you never get fed up with life's situations, do you really want to grow? Being fed up means you are going to do anything necessary to achieve greatness. Being complacent means you are ok with being average! Be fed up!

#45

(Heavy Weight)

No matter your actual size, be a heavy weight in your heart. Be a big fighter and put up a big fight today! Life, you hit like a girl!

#46

(Natural Worth)

Don't devalue yourself! It's not about how much money you have or what you have accomplished. You being the best version of yourself will speak by itself. At the moment when you were down and thought you had no being; someone or something reminded you that you were worthy. Natural worth will be seen when nothing else is.

#47

(Expect It!)

All day, every day!
You have to know you are covered!
You are blessed! There is so much
that is ahead of you! Expect it, don't
doubt it!

#48

(Be Gold)

Be something that you hardly ever see anymore. Be the last of a dying breed. Be the outcast. Be the loner. Be the one thats different. Be the valuable one. Be the irreplaceable one. BE GOLD!

#49

(Won't throw you away)

There is no mistakes, issues, setbacks etc. that will allow God to want to throw you away! Yes, people will throw you away in a heartbeat for any little reason. Remember this; you are not trash because God doesn't make that.

#50

(Atmosphere)

The one thing about your life is that IT'S YOUR LIFE! What are you speaking into it? There may be negative or positive, mediocrity or greatness or the worst or the best. You control your thoughts and the things that come out of your mouth for your well-being! What's in your Atmosphere?

#51

(Due Time)

I may not have everything I want right now but there is a thing called "due time." Even when it gets hard to see or understand, I am reminded that there is a time and a place for all things. There is no such thing as it ever being over for you. Your season is coming and your time will be due!

Checkpoint!

Every chance you get to live another day, live it to the fullest that you can. The lord blessed you with it so; he will bless you in it. Will all your days be easy? Absolutely not! Will all your days be great? NOPE! Through it all still be thankful for the days and chance you are given and learn how to live through whatever comes your way.

#52

(Count It a Victory)

If you are losing right now, don't think that you will be losing forever! At times you may hurt so bad that a win might not be in sight anywhere. At what moment will you overcome and say I will win? Your situation is what you make it. When you "count it a victory" even when it may not be yet is the moment you do win.

#53

(Why Not Me)

If they can do it then I can too! If they can have it I can too! This is the mindset to have but don't focus so much on material. Focus on the task at hand and never count yourself out! As humans we all get equal opportunity to do great things. So, the next time success is what you see point to yourself and say "WHY NOT ME!"

#54

(Arena)

Check this out: SHINE IN YOUR OWN ARENA! Did you catch that? Believe that you are the best at what it is that you do. We all have different occupations and hobbies that we do daily. How are you within the things that you do often? Are you doing it to say "look at me" or are you doing it to say "this is my ARENA!

#55

(Good Use)

Imagine that you get a package that comes in a box. Instead of you throwing the box away you keep it because you know it will come to good use. Just like life, you never know when you will be used but I hope you are ready because hopefully you will be put to good use.

#56

(Investment)

If you don't invest in yourself do you think someone else will? Translation: If you treat yourself like crap and don't believe in yourself, do you think someone else will? Everything from your relationship with God to learning how to treat others is very vital. No matter what it is you are putting in make sure it is making you better. When you strive for good others will strive for you.

#57

(Even In Trouble)

Stay in faith "even in trouble."
Keep it together "even in trouble."
Hold on to what you know "even in trouble."
After all is done, even in trouble you will receive double for the trouble!
WATCH WHAT I TELL YOU.

#58

(Not the Same)

Are you listening to people who are on your level or not? Why take advice from someone who doesn't want good things in life? If a person is not living to be the best they can be, do you really think that they can help you out? If they are not the same as you, they don't need to play the game with you.

Checkpoint!

ALWAYS REALIZE: When you are chosen…
You will experience things above the norm. You will be separated from the rest. You will see things differently than others. You will be determined to finish the race. You don't waste time on short cuts! You are chosen because you are simply set aside to be a blessing to those around you and yourself. You are the testimony! Do you accept it?

#59

(Question and Answer)

Q: How can I lose when I'm a child
of God?
A: I can't!
Don't forget that

#60

(In the drive thru)

*Place your order (Tell God what you want)
*Wait patiently for the order to be ready (The blessings are being prepared)
*Pick up your order at the window (Your blessings are ready)

God tells you to just ask at the speaker. Be still in the line of the drive thru. Receive what you have asked for or are in need of at the window. Jesus runs the whole business. He takes the request, he prepares the meats and feeds you!

Parting Words

It really warms my heart to know that you all would take the time out to read this book.

My passion is writing and helping to change lives through my personal experiences. If you were touched by this book, please read my other book *Old Soul 22*. It can be found on Amazon by searching or you can get there directly by typing in http://tinyurl.com/oldsoul22.

I would love to connect with you and continue providing positive inspiration for your daily live. You can connect with me on

Instagram @quayb

Facebook https://facebook.com/somebodyandworthy

Twitter @HumbleGuy_QB

Made in the USA
Charleston, SC
03 March 2016